after all

after all
for those who believe in love...

- terri st.cloud

bone sigh books

ISBN: 978-0-9815440-2-1 (pbk)
bone sigh arts
www.bonesigharts.com
www.bonesighbooks.com

don't steal any of this work.
if you want to use it, just ask!

cover art: yohan
www.bfg-productions.com

book layout / design:
zakk and yo
www.mazuzu.com

contents

contents

there is a power that lies
inside our hearts
that is beyond our comprehension...
it is to that power and to the
one who brought me
to its gates...
that i humbly offer this book.

there came a rough time in my life that knocked the wind right out of me... and with the wind, a lot of my beliefs.

my belief in love was the first to go.

 i walked around telling my friends that i didn't believe in love anymore, that i had serious doubts it even existed, and i just wasn't sure what to do about the whole deal. stunned with this whole view of life that had overtaken me, my friends would look at me funny, then worried, and then shake their heads. i could see the concern and confusion in their eyes, 'if terri doesn't believe in love anymore, then what's going on with the world?'

but when i questioned them about what it really was, and did they really know it or have it, some very interesting conversations unfolded.

'what is love?' became such an intensely burning question inside of me; i grabbed everyone i met and asked them for their input. it wouldn't matter where we were or what was going on, that question would come up! i got nowhere fast. no clear definitions or meanings or anything i could wrap my hands around.

but somewhere along the way, without even knowing it was happening, a shift was taking place. i went from not believing love really existed, to believing that it is the most powerful (and misunderstood) force there is.

it happened slowly, starting out when a shop owner i was working with asked me if i had any love poems i could put together for valentine's day. 'love poems?!' i thought! i don't even believe in love!! but then as i sat down to go thru my quotes, i saw that there were quite a few that dealt with love! love for friends, very special cousins, my kids, people who had helped me in my darkness, it was all right there in my writings. to my surprise, i had a lot of love in my stuff!

i think that's when i first starting opening my eyes to it again.

grudgingly, i agreed that yeah, there was love.... between friends, and definitely for my kids... but that romantic kinda love... that partner kinda stuff.... don't even get me started on that subject!

well... it wasn't long before i got "involved." ohmygosh. it was by total accident. i would never have done it on purpose! a friend who was also interested in figuring out what love is, who became a best friend.... crept his way right into my heart.

loving someone when you are so scared of love that you don't even want to admit it exists, is quite a challenge.

luckily for me, my friend was up for weathering the challenge.

i am by no means any more of an expert than when i started out years ago wondering if love even existed. all i know is that i have touched love at times, and that i have seen doorways to other worlds in that touching. i believe with my whole heart that it's the biggest force there is, that we haven't a clue of how deep it can really go, and that it's the most important thing we can learn about.

i'm convinced that you have to have an open heart to touch love. and that opening a heart – really, really opening it – is the most difficult challenge in the world. but when we do, it's pure magic!

these writings reflect part of my journey into that world of magic. it is my hope that they also reflect part of your journey.

discoveries

there was no leader.
they explored together.
asking nothing from each other but honesty,
they discovered themselves...
they discovered friendship...
they discovered real.

friendship

he asks nothing from her.
has no expectations of her.
humbly handing her wisdom
masked in his questions
he allows her growth ~
and she grows.

let's go

trembling, she opened her heart.
quietly, she whispered, 'let's go.'

you

"what is it you want?" he asked.
and she stopped.
she wasn't used to anyone asking her that.
"you..." she responded.
and they were never the same again.

commitment

it is in the commitment to trust
that mountains begin to move.
it is in the commitment to love
that walls begin to crumble,
and it is in the commitment to one's self
that worlds unimagined begin to become
real.

love

and they came to a place that demanded
their giving beyond comfort,
beyond safety,
beyond scars –
a place they longed for
and feared deeply.
they had come to love.

her kiss

you have taught me the strength of tenderness.

trust

she shared with him her innermost thoughts and
trembled.
he held them with the gentleness of love
and taught her trust.

total being

i have never felt like this before!
i want to experience it totally.
explore every corner.
open to every sensation.
go beyond the limits.
no self doubt, no inner barriers ~
total being!

thanks

who do i thank for her?
the stars?
the universe?
she herself?
none of these thanks seem enough for
such a gift as having her in my life.

pulling me in

it was her strength that attracted me to her ~
and yet it is her gentleness that holds me close.
it was her wise words i listened to ~
and yet it is her questioning that bonds me to her.
it was her belief in herself that i admired ~
and yet it is her self doubt that endears her so.
the world of opposites that spin inside her
pull me in ever deeper.
and it is in that pull that love is born.

our canoe ride

climb inside this trust we've built.
we've got walls to crash down,
barriers to break thru, and
entire universes to discover.

my partner

you are my best friend, my confidante,
my partner.
you know me unlike anyone else.
accepting me and believing in me beyond
anything i've ever experienced before.
come, let me mirror your love back to you,
holding you gently in my heart forever.

my son

i watched him carry the spider out
of the house.
talking to it as he walked.
he had no idea how brightly his
heart shone to me at that moment.

maryann

it only takes seconds.
she just proved it to me.
moments ago i had never met her.
and now, somehow,
i've known her forever.

belief

he saw more than the good in her ~
he saw her potential ~
and believed in what he saw.
it was that belief that pushed her forward.

the perfect birthday present

how do i give him the feeling i get when
his eyes twinkle at me?
if only i could return that -
and wrap it with a polka dotted bow,
ahh - then i'd have found him the perfect
birthday gift.

boxes

needing to feel safe
she had labeled him and put him in a box.
soon she found she needed honesty more than safety.
she removed the box
and found him grinning.

stories

she asked me for my story and i felt validated.
she listened to my words and i gained trust.
she shared her story and i heard wisdom.
she opened her arms and i knew love.

bonds

making my head shake in wonder
and my heart open beyond words -
it's a bond that defies logic.

reaching him

he seemed so untouchable sometimes.
so independently stubbornly out there on his own.
not sure how to reach him, she loved him with
her whole heart.
he turned towards her and loved her back.

being

how do you describe the joy of being with someone
for no other reason but to be?

letting her in

to let her in close,
deep,
where no one's been before -
this was a scary task.
but to leave her out was scarier still.

sacred ground

i want to enter your sacred ground,
to hold you in the depth of your spirit,
to be surrounded by the mists of your soul
and to soak in the essence of you.
it's a giving and a taking i honor quietly,
solemnly.
if your door is open, i am there.

fire and heart

i think we used to be one soul, she said.
but we're just too intense to be housed in one body.
you're heart and i'm fire
and we've found ourselves in each other.
heart smiled and loved fire
with all she had.

together

standing in the middle of the chaos,
we hold on tight to each other.
knowing nothing for sure
except the love between us,
we go forward.

musicians

it went beyond sharing good times and sadness,
it went beyond sharing love and passions.
what they shared was Life in its truest sense -
the opening and the flow
and the becoming more of who they were.

the magic chair

they talked late into the nite -
never looking at each other.
for it wasn't themselves they were looking for,
but what came thru them.

beyond forgiving

it's beyond forgiving you, she said.
i've done that.
it's your turn now.
you must forgive yourself.
and then together we can believe in us.
in our ability to understand,
to let go, and to grow.

all parts

trusting and allowing all parts
of herself to show up with me,
she let me love her.
and i loved all of her.
with gratitude and joy,
i loved all of her.

a blink of an eye

mortality -
shortness of life -
brevity of the moment -
i just want to hold on tight...
but all i can hold onto
is my love for you.

growing

he walked thru her hurt with her.
never leaving her side.
he wasn't afraid to look
at their struggle,
rather, he was afraid not to.
and once again
their love grew new roots.

he doesn't even know

she heard him speak his truth.
his strength inspired her.
his insights amazed her.
his kindness astounded her.
he was everything she wanted to be.

wrong verdict

"damaged goods" was the title she had given herself,
"never loving wholly," her verdict.
she'd been wrong.
her heart was totally open tonite,
her love as free as a child's.

fire everywhere

dragon roared.
heart burned.
together, they made fire everywhere.

hidden fears

always trying to be strong,
he hid his fear -
from her,
from himself.
when would he know it was okay
to be afraid -
and that they could
share that too?

where real chaos cooks

love transcends the chaos
and brings a calm.
but don't be fooled –
for in that calm
the real chaos cooks –
bubbling up our answers.

worlds unseen

like a wave,
love engulfed her –
sweeping her to worlds unseen

the only door

closing down was her protection.
it had saved her.
gotten her thu.
but now the question wasn't about saving "her" –
it was about creating "them."
and Trust was her only door.

diving

timidly reaching for it,
she touched it,
warm and encompassing,
she ran from it.
silly girl, it was okay to love.
she nodded
and dived right into it.

gone

your slightest movements occupy my mind.
a million miles away,
you make me grin.
love turns your quirks to magic –
and my heart sings.

gold

when things were tough,
he remembered who she was.
that to her was gold.

real

turning my tears to laughter
and my panic to trust,
making my darkness part of my Light,
and my wanderings part of my growth,
you love me into real.

her words

her words held me close.
her acceptance told me i mattered.
her love changed my life.

my guys

always there when i need you...
forever making me laugh...
pushing me to stretch
and opening my pools of giving –
you teach me.
and it is in your very presence that
i become gratitude.

open

"you can't close down now.
you have to open all the way," he said.
"why does it matter to you?" she asked.
"because it isn't love unless you open," he whispered.

making it thru

it's with gratitude that
we made it thru...
that we survived and learned
and loved and stumbled and
caught ourselves thru...
it's with gratitude i drink in
the sky today.
it's with gratitude i drink in you.

ed

it came in the form of a laugh.
the hug i needed so badly.
i felt the warmth surround me
it was there.
it was real.
and you were just what i needed.

in their love

it was in their love for each other
that they could become love for themselves.

her hero

he was her hero-
not in the cape flying/out the window way.
but in the best friend / believes in who you are
kinda way.

my dreams

over and over again
you remind me
not to just reach for my dreams,
but to live them.
breathe them.
become them.
and little by little,
i do.

finger tip

finger tip to finger tip,
i long to reach out to you.
to put the palm of my hand
against your skin.
i close my eyes
and imagine you're here –
and i wait for your return.

clarity

confusion and doubt
can fill my heart so easily.
until i close my eyes and think
of my love for you.
clarity and courage come into focus –
and i wait for your return.

treasure of you

gently wrapping my heart
around your glow,
i thank god for the treasure of you.

crumbling walls

opening your heart to me,
you let me in.
gently,
gratefully,
i entered…
and one more wall in the
world crumbled.

my heart

i took my heart back and made it mine.
it hurt at first....
and then it sang.

the sea

pushing hard against the walls,
she broke thru into a sea of vulnerability.
it's where she knew she had to be
if she was going to honestly know love.

one more piece

you gave me one more piece
of the world.

roots

her toes touched the roots they
were growing, and her heart smiled.

touching love

reaching for your hand,
you gently touch me back,
separateness fades,
oneness surrounds
and together we touch love.

really

if i can love you in my heart,
can i carry it down to my bones?
will my cells fill with it,
carrying it past any physical realm?
will i become love when i learn
to really love you?

yeah

yeah, they were different.
way, way different.
but when she put her fear down
and stepped into the knowing,
she didn't care anymore.
turning towards him,
she offered him belief.

my gentle giant

there is a kindness
that you carry around
gently…quietly.
when i look your way,
the light shining out of
your eyes takes my breath
away.

sometimes

sometimes all you can do is step back.
even when you wish you could jump in.
sometimes all you can do is love
from afar –
and sometimes that's where you really
touch love.

giving

maybe when you really love yourself
you can see beyond that self -
and then maybe you never give yourself away.
maybe you just give.

playing it safe

the fear won't help save what you have -
it will make you lose what you could become.

allowing it

it's not about controlling.
it's about being present,
being open,
being aware...
and allowing it to come.

knowing love

to know love,
to truly touch its depths,
i must let go of all my guards –
and drop with totalness
into vulnerability

everything

i give you my heart.
sometimes i think it's just not enough.
and then sometimes i know it's everything.

herselves

knowing now they would be seen,
her selves stood before her.
circling her in love –they claimed their
right to be.

the whole

she could never go back and make some of
the details pretty. all she could do was move
forward and make the whole beautiful.

yin yang

it was in their opposites that they
traveled the same direction.
he walked the white.
she the black.
twisting and turning into each other's realms.
stretching their hearts past single colors
into the place of all.

her offering

unwrapping her hands
from around her heart,
she offered her all.

after all

turns out she believed in love after all.

terri didn't know she was a writer, didn't know she was an artist, she just plain ol' didn't know a heck of a lot of anything. and then some good ol' fashioned, gut wrenching, heart ripping pain gripped her life, and she started to discover things about herself.

she began her journey inward. when the pain got to be too much for her, she spilled out her feelings on paper. wanting to honor those feelings somehow, she added art to them. it was with that mixing of spilling and honoring that bone sighs were born.

needing to find a way to support herself and her sons, she began peddling her watercolor bone sighs shop to shop. thru an amazing journey of tears, miracles, trust, terror, laughter, squeezing her eyes closed tight, and following her heart, somehow bone sigh arts became a real business.

home made books were offered for awhile among her prints and cards. cumbersome to make and lacking the desired quality, there came a time when the books needed to become "real." grabbing her sons, terri and the guys decided to go into print!

without terri's sons, bone sigh arts/books would never ever have become what it has. funny how the very reason for the business became what made the business successful. those boys are everything to both terri and bone sighs!

josh is the oldest. an old soul musician, born entertainer, and a loveable guy! yo yo is their gentle giant who's turning into the world's best graphic designer! and zakk is the logical one. computer geek and mad inventor with the marshmallow heart.

and! the boys have expanded into beginning their own businesses for themselves! (check out the information page for a listing of their websites!)

it's been quite a journey for them all.

terri's still scratchin' her head wonderin' if she'll ever figure any of it out! probably not....but she'll keep trying anyway!

- info -

terri st.cloud
15809 menk rd
accokeek md 20607
granolastew@gmail.com

bone sigh arts
BoneSighArts.com

bone sigh books
BoneSighBooks.com

Zakk and Yo's business
Mazuzu.com

Yohan's business
BFG-Productions.com

Josh's business
Poodleman.com